D1322487

Get Creative

JACQUELINE WILSON is one of Britain's bestselling authors, with more than 40 million books sold in the UK alone. She has won many prizes for her work, and in 2008 was appointed a Dame for services to children's literature.

NICK SHARRATT has written and illustrated many books for children and won numerous awards for his picture books. For over 25 years he has also enjoyed great success illustrating Jacqueline Wilson's books.

Visit Jacqueline's fantastic website at
www.jacquelinewilson.co.uk

Jacqueline Wilson

ILLUSTRATED BY NICK SHARRATT

Doodle

Draw

Write

Get Creative

Design

Craft

Colour

Imagine

DOUBLEDAY

DOUBLEDAY

UK | USA | Canada | Ireland | Australia
India | New Zealand | South Africa

Doubleday is part of the Penguin Random House group of companies
whose addresses can be found at global.penguinrandomhouse.com.

www.penguin.co.uk
www.puffin.co.uk
www.ladybird.co.uk

First published 2017

001

Text copyright © Jacqueline Wilson, 2017
Illustrations copyright © Nick Sharratt, 2017

The moral right of the author and illustrator has been asserted

Set in 12/17pt New Century Schoolbook by Falcon Oast Graphic Art Ltd
Printed and bound in China by Leo Paper Products Ltd.

A CIP catalogue record for this book is available from the British Library

ISBN: 978–0–857–53540–5

All correspondence to:
Doubleday
Penguin Random House Children's
80 Strand, London WC2R 0RL

Let's GET CREATIVE!

In the pages of this book you'll find
plenty of ideas for activities to get
your creative juices flowing, inspired
by Jacqueline Wilson's creative
characters. From drawing portraits
like Clover Moon, to baking and
decorating cakes like Biscuits in *Buried
Alive!*, or writing amazing stories like Em in *Clean Break*, let your
imagination guide you as you turn your ideas into reality . . .

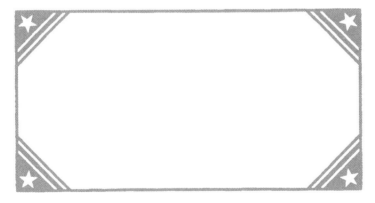

Use the spaces to write or draw a record of all the
different ways you are creative every day!

THIS BOOK BELONGS TO:

Write your name and add in a picture of yourself in the frame above –
you could draw yourself, create a collage from old magazines
or stick in a photo – be as creative as you can!

BEING CREATIVE EVERY DAY
by Jacqueline Wilson

Would you call yourself creative? I'm not just talking about writing stories. You can be creative in all kinds of different ways. Perhaps you love baking and decorating your own cakes? Maybe you knit stripy, rainbow-coloured scarves for all your friends and family. You might be good at sewing – making outfits for your little sister's dolls. Are you musical? Can you compose tunes on your recorder? Do you whirl around your bedroom making up your own dance moves?

I liked doing ALL these things when I was young. I hardly ever baked because my mum didn't want me messing up her kitchen, but I was so proud when I managed a few basic rock cakes and some cornflake crispies. I liked knitting, though I could only do purl and plain. I made scarves and patchwork squares, but somehow I never got the hang of knitting evenly, so my handiwork was very lopsided! I didn't have a little sister, though I secretly played with dolls until I was in secondary school, and had a go at making miniature dresses – but they never fitted properly. I learned the recorder at school, but couldn't stop squawking when I tried to play a tune. I frequently danced around my bedroom, but kept bumping into things.

Thank goodness I was OK at writing stories! At primary school I was bottom of the class in maths, and was hopeless at sport, though I was known as the girl who wrote good stories.

At secondary school my English teacher wasn't so keen on my work – she felt I had too chatty a style – but I didn't let her discourage me. I was still determined to be a writer, even though my teacher and my parents thought this a ridiculous idea.

My teenage diaries make constant reference to my writing. I started a new 'novel' every week, and was busy planning a proper writing career. It was a joyful triumph when, at the age of seventeen, I managed to get my first short story published. I trained as a magazine journalist and learned the most important thing about writing: discipline! Journalists can't afford to have writer's block. They have to write whether they feel like it or not. They must deliver articles on time or the editor will get rid of them.

So right from the start of my career I developed a regular writing habit. I write every single day – even Christmas Day, though I admit this is a bit weird! I find it works best if I start when I wake up. I feed the cat, take the dog into the garden, make myself a cup of coffee, and then hop back into bed in my pyjamas. I open up my laptop and get stuck into my story – and usually, after an hour or so, I've written about 1,000 words.

I don't expect you to do that! When you're young you can write whenever you feel like it – maybe just a couple of paragraphs at a time. You don't have to finish a story if you get bored. You don't have to plan it all out. It's supposed to be fun. But writing regularly will help you enormously if you want to be an author when you grow up.

Jacqueline Wilson

BEING CREATIVE EVERY DAY
by Nick Sharratt

I do believe that I managed to be creative every day, one way or another, when I was a boy. I loved drawing of course, and I always had a picture on the go. Often I would buy a large sheet of paper from the stationer's and, using my felt-tip pens, draw character after character, gradually filling the paper with a really busy crowd scene. The radio would be on, I'd have a bag of sherbet lemons or pineapple chunks to hand, and I'd be in heaven. I tried creating pictures in all kinds of media: crayons, pastels, poster paints, watercolours, oils, scraper board (all my hard-earned paper-round money went on art materials), but I always felt happiest drawing with felt-tips.

I was an enthusiastic model-maker too and made loads of things, puppets in particular, out of modelling clay or plasticine or papier mâché. I was pretty good at constructing little stage sets from bits of cardboard, and one of my dad's work colleagues even made me a simple wooden theatre to display them.

Photography was another passion and, despite the fact that my camera was not much more than a toy, I still managed to come second in a photography competition. (I'd snapped my brother and sisters kitted out in dressing-up clothes, pretending to be various crazy characters.) Imagine how thrilled I was to go on a children's TV programme to collect my prize.

I was always jazzing up my bedroom with massive collages of pictures cut out from magazines, complicated hanging mobiles or wall decorations made out of coloured paper and kitchen foil, all stuck up with Blu Tack. When I was thirteen my parents finally allowed me to paint a big mural over two walls of my room, the main feature of which was a huge orange sun with bright yellow rays rising up behind green hills painted just above my bed. Cool!

I had a lot of fun being a youngster with a vivid imagination and a head full of ideas that I just had to try out. And I was very lucky to have a mum and dad who encouraged me with my artistic endeavours and didn't mind too much about the 'creative mess' that was my bedroom and all the modelling clay I trod into the carpet!

Nick Sharratt

JANUARY

Many people like to make new year's resolutions
in January ~ why not make being creative every day
one of yours? Don't forget to write down what
you get up to in the space provided.

♥ MY RESOLUTIONS ♥

....
....
....
....
....
....
....
....
....
....
....
....

♥ 1 JANUARY ♥ ....

....

....

....

....

....

....

....

....

♥ 2 JANUARY ♥ ....

....

....

....

....

....

....

....

....

♥ 3 JANUARY ♥ ....

....

....

....

....

....

....

....

....

....

♥ 4 JANUARY ♥ ....

....

....

....

....

....

....

....

....

♥ 5 JANUARY ♥ ....

....

....

....

....

....

....

....

....

♥ 6 JANUARY ♥ ....

....

....

....

....

....

....

....

♥ 7 JANUARY ♥ ....
....
....
....
....
....
....
....
....
....

♥ 8 JANUARY ♥ ....
....
....
....
....
....
....
....
....
....

♥ 9 JANUARY ♥ ....

....

....

....

....

....

....

....

....

....

♥ 10 JANUARY ♥ ....

....

....

....

....

....

....

....

....

....

Let's GET CREATIVE . . .
On the Page

In *The Story of Tracy Beaker*, Tracy decorates the pages of her life story with funny drawings and doodles. Use the instructions below to draw Tracy, then why not grab a piece of paper and have a go at drawing yourself in a similarly strong pose?

Give her lots of springy curls.

Tracy's got her hands on her hips to make herself look important.

Tracy is never afraid to let her imagination run wild and loves nothing more than imagining herself in exciting situations. In the space below, make up a thrilling story starring you. Like Tracy, illustrate your tale with nifty line drawings of your special adventure!

TRACY BEAKER'S story continues in *The Dare Game* and in her third adventure, *Starring Tracy Beaker*, Tracy gets a leading role in the school play. Turn to the end of the April section to join in the drama . . .

....

....

....

....

....

....

....

....

....

....

....

....

....

....

....

....

....

♥ 13 JANUARY ♥ ....

....

....

....

....

....

....

....

....

....

....

♥ 14 JANUARY ♥ ....

....

....

....

....

....

....

....

....

....

♥ 15 JANUARY ♥ ....
....
....
....
....
....
....
....
....
....

♥ 16 JANUARY ♥ ....
....
....
....
....
....
....
....
....
....

♥ 17 JANUARY ♥ ....

....

....

....

....

....

....

....

....

♥ 18 JANUARY ♥ ....

....

....

....

....

....

....

....

....

....

♥ 19 JANUARY ♥ ....

....

....

....

....

....

....

....

....

♥ 20 JANUARY ♥ ....

....

....

....

....

....

....

....

....

♥ 21 JANUARY ♥ ....

....

....

....

....

....

....

....

....

♥ 22 JANUARY ♥ ....

....

....

....

....

....

....

....

....

....

♥ 23 JANUARY ♥ ....

....
....
....
....
....
....
....
....
....
....

♥ 24 JANUARY ♥ ....

....
....
....
....
....
....
....
....

♥ 25 JANUARY ♥ ....

....

....

....

....

....

....

....

....

....

♥ 26 JANUARY ♥ ....

....

....

....

....

....

....

....

....

....

....

♥ 27 JANUARY ♥ ....

....

....

....

....

....

....

....

....

....

♥ 28 JANUARY ♥ ....

....

....

....

....

....

....

....

....

....

♥ 29 JANUARY ♥ ....

....

....

....

....

....

....

....

....

♥ 30 JANUARY ♥ ....

....

....

....

....

....

....

....

....

....

....

....

....

....

....

....

....

....

I wanted to stay in my nightie and sit up in bed and stick stuff in my scrapbook. Ms Balsam had given me lots of her magazines. I was having fun snipping out heads and bodies and arms and legs and making new people on my page. Sometimes I invented strange new species with six arms or car wheels for feet.

LOLA ROSE

Jayni in *Lola Rose* loves to collect and cut out pictures from magazines to make creative collages for her precious scrapbook. Use the facing page to make a collage by gluing in images you have found. Will your creation be weird and wonderful or decorative and pretty?

MY SCRAPBOOK

FEBRUARY

Have you managed to keep up with your creative
resolutions? Write about your progress below – you
could even add some new ones to the list!

....

....

....

....

....

....

....

....

....

....

....

....

....

....

....

♥ 1 FEBRUARY ♥ ....
....
....
....
....
....
....
....
....

♥ 2 FEBRUARY ♥ ....
....
....
....
....
....
....
....
....

♥ 3 FEBRUARY ♥ ....

....

....

....

....

....

....

....

....

....

♥ 4 FEBRUARY ♥ ....

....

....

....

....

....

....

....

....

....

♥ 5 FEBRUARY ♥ ....

....

....

....

....

....

....

....

....

....

♥ 6 FEBRUARY ♥ ....

....

....

....

....

....

....

....

....

....

♥ 7 FEBRUARY ♥ ....

....

....

....

....

....

....

....

....

....

♥ 8 FEBRUARY ♥ ....

....

....

....

....

....

....

....

....

....

♥ 9 FEBRUARY ♥ ....

....

....

....

....

....

....

....

....

♥ 10 FEBRUARY ♥ ....

....

....

....

....

....

....

....

....

Let's GET CREATIVE . . . With Creatures

I draw a killer whale first, doing a lot of shading so that it looks properly black and white. It looks more like a smiley penguin than a whale, so I draw its mouth open, with a row of vicious-looking teeth, and half a baby sea lion sticking out. I do a little speech bubble: 'I am a killer whale and I am killing.'
THE LONGEST WHALE SONG

The more amazing facts Ella learns about whales, the more she's inspired to draw pictures of them in their (not so) natural habitat! Seas and oceans are mysterious places, and scientists still haven't discovered all the different species that live in their watery depths. Using what you know about sea-dwelling animals, on the page opposite, can you draw a picture of a creature from your imagination that calls the sea its home?

Write down five fun facts about your fantastical underwater creation on the lines below.

1. ....

2. ....

3. ....

4. ....

5. ....

Jacqueline Wilson did lots of research to write *The Longest Whale Song*.

SHE SAYS: *I listened, fascinated, to recordings of whale songs. They sound very strange and melancholy. It's odd to think that at this very moment, somewhere out in the ocean, there are whales singing.*

♥ 11 FEBRUARY ♥ ....

....

....

....

....

....

....

....

....

....

....

♥ 12 FEBRUARY ♥ ....

....

....

....

....

....

....

....

....

....

....

♥ 13 FEBRUARY ♥ ....

....

....

....

....

....

....

....

....

♥ 14 FEBRUARY ♥ ....

....

....

....

....

....

....

....

....

....

♥ 15 FEBRUARY ♥ ....

....

....

....

....

....

....

....

....

....

♥ 16 FEBRUARY ♥ ....

....

....

....

....

....

....

....

....

....

♥ 17 FEBRUARY ♥ ....
....
....
....
....
....
....
....
....
....
....

♥ 18 FEBRUARY ♥ ....
....
....
....
....
....
....
....
....
....
....

♥ 19 FEBRUARY ♥ ....

....

....

....

....

....

....

....

....

♥ 20 FEBRUARY ♥ ....

....

....

....

....

....

....

....

♥ 21 FEBRUARY ♥ ....

....

....

....

....

....

....

....

....

♥ 22 FEBRUARY ♥ ....

....

....

....

....

....

....

....

....

....

Let's GET CREATIVE . . .
With Faces!

Perhaps I could save up for some proper paints and a brush and do a portrait of Megs on the wall. I could picture it now: I'd have her sitting on the floor with her arms round her knees, her head on one side, smiling shyly at me. I'd work slowly, with a fine brush, making it such a true portrait that it would look as if Megs were really there in the room with me. I'd see her first thing every morning when I opened my eyes and last thing every night when I drifted off to sleep.

CLOVER MOON

Use the space inside the frame on the page opposite to draw a portrait of someone who is important to you. If it's possible, get them to sit in front of you, or why not try to picture their face in your mind and draw or paint them from memory?

♥ 23 FEBRUARY ♥ ....
....
....
....
....
....
....
....
....
....

♥ 24 FEBRUARY ♥ ....
....
....
....
....
....
....
....
....
....

♥ 25 FEBRUARY ♥ ....

....

....

....

....

....

....

....

....

....

♥ 26 FEBRUARY ♥ ....

....

....

....

....

....

....

....

....

....

♥ 27 FEBRUARY ♥ ....

....

....

....

....

....

....

....

....

♥ 28 FEBRUARY ♥ ....

....

....

....

....

....

....

....

....

....
....
....
....
....
....
....
....
....

If it's a leap year, enjoy an extra day to be creative!

In *The Bed and Breakfast Star* Elsa keeps herself amused by making up jokes. Why not have a go at coming up with a wisecrack of your own? Write it down in the space below.

MARCH

Have you managed to keep up with your creative resolutions? Write about your progress below – you could even add some new ones to the list!

....
....
....
....
....
....
....
....
....
....
....
....
....
....
....

♥ 1 MARCH ♥ ....

....

....

....

....

....

....

....

....

....

♥ 2 MARCH ♥ ....

....

....

....

....

....

....

....

....

....

♥ 3 MARCH ♥ ....

....

....

....

....

....

....

....

....

....

♥ 4 MARCH ♥ ....

....

....

....

....

....

....

....

....

....

♥ 5 MARCH ♥ ....

....

....

....

....

....

....

....

....

....

♥ 7 MARCH ♥ ....
....
....
....
....
....
....
....
....

♥ 8 MARCH ♥ ....
....
....
....
....
....
....
....
....

♥ 9 MARCH ♥ ....

....

....

....

....

....

....

....

....

....

♥ 10 MARCH ♥ ....

....

....

....

....

....

....

....

....

....

....

....

....

....

....

....

....

....

....

I wouldn't mind my story being written up in some magazine. A book would be better of course, but maybe that could come later.

THE STORY OF TRACY BEAKER

Use the space opposite to design the cover for a book you'd like to write. Does it have a brilliant title? And would you write under your own name or a pseudonym?

♥ 12 MARCH ♥ ....

....

....

....

....

....

....

....

....

....

♥ 13 MARCH ♥ ....

....

....

....

....

....

....

....

....

....

♥ 14 MARCH ♥ ....

....

....

....

....

....

....

....

....

....

....

♥ 15 MARCH ♥ ....

....

....

....

....

....

....

....

....

....

....

....

....

....

....

....

....

....

....

....

....

♥ 17 MARCH ♥ ....

....

....

....

....

....

....

....

....

♥ **18 MARCH** ♥ ....

....

....

....

....

....

....

....

....

....

....

♥ **19 MARCH** ♥ ....

....

....

....

....

....

....

....

....

....

....

Let's GET CREATIVE . . . With Stories

Having published well over 100 books, Jacqueline Wilson knows a thing or two about writing brilliant stories. These are her top five tips for every budding writer:

1. GET IDEAS: Everyone gets their ideas in different ways. I saw a heavily tattooed woman with her two small daughters in Central Park, and my own daughter Emma whispered that they looked like the sort of family I'd write about. That's how I came to write *The Illustrated Mum*. Another time I saw photos of children needing foster parents in my local newspaper – this gave me the idea for *The Story of Tracy Beaker*. Occasionally other people give me ideas; the Director of the Foundling Museum asked me if I'd ever consider writing a book about a foundling child – and *Hetty Feather* sprang to life.

2. CREATE CHARACTERS: The most important part of writing a story is getting to know your characters and making them seem real. Did you ever have imaginary friends when you were little? Creating new characters is a similar process. Hold conversations with your characters in your head. Don't just think about their looks; what are your characters like inside? What are their likes and dislikes? Who is important to them? Think it all through and make notes. You probably won't need to put half these things in your story, but thinking carefully about them will help make your characters come alive on the page.

3. START YOUR STORY: I don't think you need several paragraphs of description and explanation before you get started on the story. Jump straight in. My tip would be to pretend you've got the most amazing piece of news and you're dashing into school to tell your best friend all about it, and you just have to seize hold of them and give them the whole story straight away, making it as amusing and astonishing as possible so that you keep their full attention.

4. MAKE SOMETHING HAPPEN: It doesn't matter what sort of story you write, it's good to have a bit of conflict – a bit of a struggle, something going wrong or something surprising – that your main character has to try and sort out. A princess might be locked up in a castle and she has to escape. A boy has lost his dog and has to find him. A dinosaur is suddenly spotted walking down the street, nibbling the treetops. It's up to you to let the story evolve. Sometimes it's good to work it all out beforehand so you don't get stuck halfway through. But other times it works to write at white-hot speed and see what happens without planning anything at all. If you've got started on your story but are stuck in the middle, try talking inside your head to your main character. Ask them what would really worry them. Then write it down and see how they cope.

5. END YOUR STORY: This is the best bit. You've written and written, and now you've nearly finished the story. You can't wait to write THE END after the last line. It's a terrible temptation to hurry things along, because if you're anything like me, you just want to be finished with the whole thing. I used to find I wrote the last few pages of my stories too quickly, but now I try to give the last chapter even more time and attention than the first. I try to round everything off in a satisfying way, but that doesn't mean I always spell everything out. Sometimes I deliberately leave my readers to work out what's going to happen next, though I always give a heavy hint. I like to keep all the options open – but if you find my endings disconcerting, you're always free to write your own versions.

So, let's say you've taken your time over your ending and are pleased with your story. I'm afraid you've still got a little work to do, especially if it's a story for school, for a special project or for a competition. Read it through. See if there are parts that don't seem very important, or simply a bit boring. How can you improve them? Could you pop something new in that will make your story seem more interesting? Have you checked all your spellings and remembered all your punctuation? It can seem like this is very tedious, but it's often only when I've got to this stage that a really good idea occurs to me. I don't like rewriting – but it's generally vitally necessary. You want your story to be as good as possible, don't you?

♥ 20 MARCH ♥ ....

....

....

....

....

....

....

....

....

....

....

♥ 21 MARCH ♥ ....

....

....

....

....

....

....

....

....

♥ 22 MARCH ♥ ....

....

....

....

....

....

....

....

....

SCREELH!!!

♥ 23 MARCH ♥ ....

....

....

....

....

....

....

....

....

....

....

♥ 24 MARCH ♥ ....

....

....

....

....

....

....

....

....

....

♥ 25 MARCH ♥ ....

....

....

....

....

....

....

....

....

♥ 26 MARCH ♥ ....

....

....

....

....

....

....

....

....

....

♥ 27 MARCH ♥ ....

....

....

....

....

....

....

....

....

....

♥ 28 MARCH ♥ ....

....

....

....

....

....

....

....

....

♥ 29 MARCH ♥ ....

....

....

....

....

....

....

....

....

♥ 30 MARCH ♥ ....

....

....

....

....

....

....

....

....

♥ 31 MARCH ♥ ....

....

....

....

....

....

....

....

APRIL

Have you managed to keep up with your creative resolutions? Write about your progress below – you could even add some new ones to the list!

....

....

....

....

....

....

....

....

....

....

....

....

....

....

♥ 1 APRIL ♥ ....

....

....

....

....

....

....

....

....

♥ 2 APRIL ♥ ....

....

....

....

....

....

....

....

....

....

♥ 3 APRIL ♥ ....

....

....

....

....

....

....

....

....

....

♥ 4 APRIL ♥ ....

....

....

....

....

....

....

....

....

♥ 5 APRIL ♥ ....

....

....

....

....

....

....

....

....

....

♥ 6 APRIL ♥ ....

....

....

....

....

....

....

....

....

....

♥ 7 APRIL ♥ ....

....

....

....

....

....

....

....

....

♥ 8 APRIL ♥ ....

....

....

....

....

....

....

....

....

♥ 9 APRIL ♥ ....

....

....

....

....

....

....

....

....

....

♥ 10 APRIL ♥ ....

....

....

....

....

....

....

....

....

....

♥ 11 APRIL ♥ ....

....

....

....

....

....

....

....

....

....

♥ 12 APRIL ♥ ....

....

....

....

....

....

....

....

....

....

♥ 13 APRIL ♥ ....

....

....

....

....

....

....

....

....

....

♥ 14 APRIL ♥ ....

....

....

....

....

....

....

....

....

....

....

Let's GET CREATIVE ...
In the Kitchen

Biscuits carefully carried a big plate into the garden,
candles flickering. It was a brown cake, but it wasn't any
old ordinary chocolate cake. It had a little roof! . . .
'It's a wishing well,' said Biscuits. 'You get the biggest
birthday wish when you blow your candles out – and
then every single slice has a special wish in it too.'
BEST FRIENDS

Once you've mastered the basics in the kitchen, baking is
a brilliant way to exercise your imagination and make
something new. Follow the recipe to make cupcakes with the
help of a grown-up – why not add a twist to the flavours
or decorations to create a uniquely delicious treat?

♥ BISCUITS'S BIRTHDAY CUPCAKES ♥

Ingredients
200g butter or margarine
200g caster sugar
200g self-raising flour
2 large eggs
2 tsp vanilla extract

Method

1. With the help of a grown-up, heat the oven to 180°C. Place a paper case in each hole of a 12-hole bun tray.

2. In a mixing bowl, using a wooden spoon, cream together the butter (or margarine) and sugar until the mixture is pale and fluffy. Carefully sift in the flour.

3. In a separate bowl, break the two eggs, taking care to remove any bits of shell. Gently beat together the eggs and the vanilla extract with a fork, then add the mixture to the flour, butter and sugar. Mix everything together to make a smooth, soft batter.

4. Spoon the batter to half-fill each of the paper cases in the tray. With the help of a grown-up, put the tray in the oven for about 20 minutes, or until the cakes are risen and golden brown.

5. Remove from the oven and transfer to a cooling rack. When they're cool, they're ready to decorate!

Why not try stirring dried fruit, nuts or chocolate chips into the batter before spooning into the paper cases? Citrus fruit flavours work brilliantly well too – instead of the vanilla extract, add the grated zest and juice of one lemon or half an orange to the mixture.

BISCUITS also pops up in *Cliffhanger* and *Buried Alive!* – if you like to laugh, you'll love reading all about what he gets up to in these adventures, as told by his best friend, Tim.

♥ **15 APRIL** ♥ ....

....

....

....

....

....

....

....

....

♥ **16 APRIL** ♥ ....

....

....

....

....

....

....

....

....

♥ 17 APRIL ♥ ....

....

....

....

....

....

....

....

....

....

....

♥ 18 APRIL ♥ ....

....

....

....

....

....

....

....

....

....

♥ 19 APRIL ♥ ....

....

....

....

....

....

....

....

....

....

♥ 20 APRIL ♥ ....

....

....

....

....

....

....

....

....

♥ 21 APRIL ♥ ....

....

....

....

....

....

....

....

....

....

♥ 22 APRIL ♥ ....

....

....

....

....

....

....

....

....

....

♥ 23 APRIL ♥ ....

....

....

....

....

....

....

....

....

....

♥ 24 APRIL ♥ ....

....

....

....

....

....

....

....

....

....

♥ 25 APRIL ♥ ....

....

....

....

....

....

....

....

....

....

♥ 26 APRIL ♥ ....

....

....

....

....

....

....

....

....

....

....

Let's GET CREATIVE . . . On the Stage!

Tears rolled down my cheeks. I don't ever cry. But I wasn't being Tracy Beaker; I was acting Scrooge, and doing it so well I heard several snuffles in the audience. They were moved to tears too by my brilliant performance!
STARRING TRACY BEAKER

In *Starring Tracy Beaker* Tracy finally gets the lead role she feels she's always deserved when she stars in the school play. Being creative on the stage can be so much fun because you get to work with lots of people, each with their own special skills: actors, designers, playwrights, directors and even musicians. A play can be written, directed and acted by the same person, while big West End productions employ a cast and crew of hundreds! Using some of the ideas below, and maybe with some help from your friends, can you create a piece of theatre to rival Tracy's school production of *A Christmas Carol*?

SCRIPT

Most plays require at least one actor to tell the story using the play's script. Have a go at writing a script. It should contain all the dialogue – the words you need the actors to say to tell the story, as well as stage directions – your instructions for the actors and the director.

COSTUMES AND PROPS

Interesting costumes can really help your actors get into character – how can you use clothes and accessories to make your play come to life? Think about how a character's clothes can give the audience more information about them – for example, does one of your characters wear a hat that they take off when they're feeling nervous? Props are objects that the actors use to make the situation seem more real: a journalist might have a notepad and pen to record interviews with.

SET

You may not have a big stage where you can perform your amazing play, but how does the space you've chosen help to tell your story? How will your actors move into and out of the performance space?

Now that everyone has learned their lines, it's time to put on your show! A play needs an audience – why not invite your friends and family to see the brilliant play you've created?

♥ 27 APRIL ♥ ....

....

....

....

....

....

....

....

....

♥ 28 APRIL ♥ ....

....

....

....

....

....

....

....

....

♥ 29 APRIL ♥ ....

....

....

....

....

....

....

....

....

♥ 30 APRIL ♥ ....

....

....

....

....

....

....

....

....

....

MAY

Have you managed to keep up with your creative
resolutions? Write about your progress below – you
could even add some new ones to the list!

....
....
....
....
....
....
....
....
....
....

....
....
....
....
....

♥ 1 MAY ♥ ....

....

....

....

....

....

....

....

....

♥ 2 MAY ♥ ....

....

....

....

....

....

....

....

....

♥ 3 MAY ♥ ....

....

....

....

....

....

....

....

....

♥ 4 MAY ♥ ....

....

....

....

....

....

....

....

....

♥ 5 MAY ♥ ....

....

....

....

....

....

....

....

....

....

♥ 6 MAY ♥ ....

....

....

....

....

....

....

....

....

....

♥ 7 MAY ♥ ....

....

....

....

....

....

....

....

....

....

♥ 8 MAY ♥ ....

....

....

....

....

....

....

....

....

'The Great Tanglefield Travelling Circus. Observe Elijah, the largest elephant in the entire world. See the exotic animals in our vast menagerie. Gasp at Fair Flora dancing on the tightrope for your delight. Chortle at the antics of Chino the Comic Clown. Marvel at Madame Adeline and her star troupe of horses. Hurrah for Tanglefield's Travelling Circus!'

HETTY FEATHER

The Great Tanglefield Circus comes to be very important in the life of one Hetty Feather. Use the space below to create a poster for your very own circus.

♥ 9 MAY ♥ ....

....

....

....

....

....

....

....

....

♥ 10 MAY ♥ ....

....

....

....

....

....

....

....

....

♥ 11 MAY ♥ ....

....

....

....

....

....

....

....

....

♥ 12 MAY ♥ ....

....

....

....

....

....

....

....

....

♥ 15 MAY ♥ ....

....

....

....

....

....

....

....

....

....

♥ 16 MAY ♥ ....

....

....

....

....

....

....

....

....

....

♥ 17 MAY ♥ ....
....
....
....
....
....
....
....
....

♥ 18 MAY ♥ ....
....
....
....
....
....
....
....
....

♥ 19 MAY ♥ ....

....

....

....

....

....

....

....

....

♥ 20 MAY ♥ ....

....

....

....

....

....

....

....

....

....

Let's GET CREATIVE . . .
On the Plate!

The wedding meal was being served: melon and Parma ham, then spaghetti carbonara, then chicken with green beans and sauté potatoes, and then delicious creamy tiramisu, with coffee and little amaretti biscuits. I could hardly move after eating all that, and I breathed shallowly so I wouldn't strain the seams of my bridesmaid's dress too much.

RENT A BRIDESMAID

Tilly gets treated to all sorts of delicious food at the many weddings she attends in Rent a Bridesmaid. Special occasions often call for special food – on the facing page, why not have a go at drawing all the delicious food you would have at a celebratory feast. Are you going to include an extravagant cake?

♥ 21 MAY ♥ ....

....

....

....

....

....

....

....

....

....

....

♥ 22 MAY ♥ ....

....

....

....

....

....

....

....

....

....

....

♥ 23 MAY ♥ ....

....

....

....

....

....

....

....

....

....

....

....

♥ 24 MAY ♥ ....

....

....

....

....

....

....

....

....

....

....

....

♥ 25 MAY ♥ ....

....

....

....

....

....

....

....

....

....

♥ 26 MAY ♥ ....

....

....

....

....

....

....

....

....

....

♥ 27 MAY ♥ ....

....

....

....

....

....

....

....

....

♥ 28 MAY ♥ ....

....

....

....

....

....

....

....

....

♥ 29 MAY ♥ ....

....

....

....

....

....

....

....

....

♥ 30 MAY ♥ ....

....

....

....

....

....

....

....

....

....

....

....

....

....

....

....

....

....

The first seven chapters of *Bad Girls* are named after the seven colours of the rainbow. Use this space to create your own rainbow – how many colours would it have in it? And which colours would they be?

JUNE

Have you managed to keep up with your creative resolutions? Write about your progress below – you could even add some new ones to the list!

....
....
....
....
....
....
....
....
....
....
....
....
....
....

♥ 1 JUNE ♥ ....

....

....

....

....

....

....

....

....

♥ 2 JUNE ♥ ....

....

....

....

....

....

....

....

....

♥ 3 JUNE ♥ ....
....
....
....
....
....
....
....
....
....

♥ 4 JUNE ♥ ....
....
....
....
....
....
....
....
....
....

♥ 5 JUNE ♥ ....

....

....

....

....

....

....

....

....

....

♥ 6 JUNE ♥ ....

....

....

....

....

....

....

....

....

♥ 7 JUNE ♥ ....

....

....

....

....

....

....

....

....

♥ 8 JUNE ♥ ....

....

....

....

....

....

....

....

....

♥ 9 JUNE ♥ ....

....

....

....

....

....

....

....

....

....

♥ 10 JUNE ♥ ....

....

....

....

....

....

....

....

....

....

Let's GET DOUBLY CREATIVE . . .

We're identical. There's very few people who can tell us apart. Well, until we start talking. I tend to go on and on. Garnet is much quieter. *That's because I can't get a word in edgeways.*
DOUBLE ACT

As well as being identical twins, Ruby and Garnet are best friends who do everything together. Why not have a go at creating a twin portrait – holding a pen or a pencil in each hand, see if you can draw a picture of a person on this page and the facing page at the same time!

JACQUELINE SAYS: I've always been fascinated by identical twins. It must be so weird looking at another person exactly like yourself. Some twins invent their own language when they're very little and get wrapped up in their own private twin-world. I wanted to write about this.

♥ 11 JUNE ♥ ....

....

....

....

....

....

....

....

....

....

♥ 12 JUNE ♥ ....

....

....

....

....

....

....

....

....

....

♥ 13 JUNE ♥ ....

....

....

....

....

....

....

....

....

....

♥ 14 JUNE ♥ ....

....

....

....

....

....

....

....

....

....

♥ 15 JUNE ♥ ....

....

....

....

....

....

....

....

....

....

♥ 16 JUNE ♥ ....

....

....

....

....

....

....

....

....

....

♥ 17 JUNE ♥ ....

....

....

....

....

....

....

....

....

....

....

....

♥ 18 JUNE ♥ ....

....

....

....

....

....

....

....

....

....

....

....

♥ 19 JUNE ♥ ....

....

....

....

....

....

....

....

....

....

♥ 20 JUNE ♥ ....

....

....

....

....

....

....

....

....

....

♥ 21 JUNE ♥ ....
....
....
....
....
....
....
....
....

♥ 22 JUNE ♥ ....
....
....
....
....
....
....
....
....

Let's GET CREATIVE . . .
With Times Past

I flipped through it furiously – and then stopped. There was a photo of this girl about my age. She even looked a bit like me, skinny and pale. It was a black-and-white photo so it was hard to make out if her hair was red too. It was long, like mine, but scraped back tight behind her ears, with a little white cap crammed on top. She was surrounded by little kids, but they weren't her brothers and sisters. She was a nursery maid. She had to look after them. She was their servant.

THE LOTTIE PROJECT

When Charlie has to write about the Victorians for a school project, she thinks it sounds really boring. But finding a photo of a girl not so different from herself sparks her imagination, and she's inspired to write the story of a Victorian nursemaid.

Imagine you lived in a different period of history – what would your name be? Where would you live? Who would your friends be? What would you do together for fun? On the facing page, create a 'photograph' of your imagined past self and write an extract from your diary on the day the picture was taken.

♥ 23 JUNE ♥ ....
....
....
....
....
....
....
....
....
....

♥ 24 JUNE ♥ ....
....
....
....
....
....
....
....
....
....
....

♥ 25 JUNE ♥ ....

....

....

....

....

....

....

....

....

....

♥ 26 JUNE ♥ ....

....

....

....

....

....

....

....

....

....

♥ 27 JUNE ♥ ....

....

....

....

....

....

....

....

....

♥ 28 JUNE ♥ ....

....

....

....

....

....

....

....

....

....

♥ 29 JUNE ♥ ....

....

....

....

....

....

....

....

....

♥ 30 JUNE ♥ ....

....

....

....

....

....

....

....

....

JULY

Have you managed to keep up with your creative resolutions? Write about your progress below - you could even add some new ones to the list!

....

....

....

....

....

....

....

....

....

....

....

....

....

♥ 1 JULY ♥ ....

....

....

....

....

....

....

....

....

....

♥ 2 JULY ♥ ....

....

....

....

....

....

....

....

....

....

♥ 3 JULY ♥

....

....

....

....

....

....

....

....

....

....

♥ 4 JULY ♥

....

....

....

....

....

....

....

....

....

....

♥ 5 JULY ♥ ....

....

....

....

....

....

....

....

....

....

♥ 6 JULY ♥ ....

....

....

....

....

....

....

....

....

....

Let's GET CREATIVE . . .
With Wishes

**The Psammead smiled at me benevolently.
'You would like a wish today then, children?' it said.
'Yes, please. It's my turn and I'd very much like to wish that
we could all fly. Please. If you're feeling particularly
obliging. I jolly well hope you are,' said Smash.**
FOUR CHILDREN AND IT

The sand fairy, the Psammead, grants the four children's
wishes but, as Rosalind knows from reading E. Nesbit's
book *Five Children and It*, the wishes always stop working
after sunset. If you could have a wish that came true for
just one day, what would it be? Draw or describe your
fantastical experience in the space below.

♥ 7 JULY ♥ ....

....

....

....

....

....

....

....

....

♥ 8 JULY ♥ ....

....

....

....

....

....

....

....

....

♥ 9 JULY ♥ ....

....

....

....

....

....

....

....

....

....

♥ 10 JULY ♥ ....

....

....

....

....

....

....

....

....

♥ 11 JULY ♥ ....

....

....

....

....

....

....

....

....

....

♥ 12 JULY ♥ ....

....

....

....

....

....

....

....

....

....

♥ 13 JULY ♥ ....

....

....

....

....

....

....

....

....

....

♥ 14 JULY ♥ ....

....

....

....

....

....

....

....

....

♥ 15 JULY ♥ ....
....
....
....
....
....
....
....
....
....

♥ 16 JULY ♥ ....
....
....
....
....
....
....
....
....
....
....

♥ 17 JULY ♥ ....
....
....
....
....
....
....

....
....
....

♥ 18 JULY ♥ ....
....
....
....
....
....
....
....
....
....

♥ 19 JULY ♥ ....
....
....
....
....
....
....
....
....
....

♥ 20 JULY ♥ ....
....
....
....
....
....
....
....
....
....

Let's GET CREATIVE . . .
with Fashion

Each mannequin stood serenely in her own window, white arms outstretched as if bestowing queenly blessings on passers-by. The one on the left was dressed in a blue and violet gown with extraordinary huge sleeves. They made such a statement that the rest of the dress was restrained, almost subdued. It was breathtakingly effective.
LITTLE STARS

Hetty's eye for detail and skill with a needle helps her to convince Miss Gibson to give her and Diamond a place to stay while they make a name for themselves in the competitive world of the Victorian music hall.

On the facing page, design a Victorian dress to go in the window of Miss Gibson's beautiful shop. Will your design be sleek and elegant? Or embroidered and showy?

♥ 21 JULY ♥ ....

....

....

....

....

....

....

....

....

....

♥ 22 JULY ♥ ....

....

....

....

....

....

....

....

....

....

♥ 23 JULY ♥ ....
....
....
....
....
....
....
....
....
....

♥ 24 JULY ♥ ....
....
....
....
....
....
....
....
....
....
....

♥ 25 JULY ♥ ....

....

....

....

....

....

....

....

....

....

♥ 26 JULY ♥ ....

....

....

....

....

....

....

....

....

....

♥ 27 JULY ♥ ....

....

....

....

....

....

....

....

....

....

♥ 28 JULY ♥ ....

....

....

....

....

....

....

....

....

....

♥ 29 JULY ♥ ....

....

....

....

....

....

....

....

....

♥ 30 JULY ♥ ....

....

....

....

....

....

....

....

....

....

....

....

....

....

....

....

....

Imagine you're a magnificent butterfly who has visited lots of flowers in Tina and Selma's butterfly garden in *The Butterfly Club*. Which flower is your favourite? Draw it here!

AUGUST

Have you managed to keep up with your creative resolutions? Write about your progress below – you could even add some new ones to the list!

....
....
....
....
....
....
....
....
....
....
....
....
....
....

♥ 1 AUGUST ♥ ....
....
....
....
....
....
....
....
....
....

♥ 2 AUGUST ♥ ....
....
....
....
....
....
....
....
....
....

♥ 3 AUGUST ♥ ....
....
....
....
....
....
....
....
....
....

♥ 4 AUGUST ♥ ....
....
....
....
....
....
....
....
....
....

♥ 5 AUGUST ♥ ....
....
....
....
....
....
....
....
....
....

♥ 6 AUGUST ♥ ....
....
....
....
....
....
....
....
....
....

♥ 7 AUGUST ♥ ....

....

....

....

....

....

....

....

....

....

♥ 8 AUGUST ♥ ....

....

....

....

....

....

....

....

....

♥ 9 AUGUST ♥ ....

....

....

....

....

....

....

....

....

♥ 10 AUGUST ♥ ....

....

....

....

....

....

....

....

....

....

Let's GET CREATIVE . . .
In Another World

I wonder what it's like for you, drawing and painting your magic world all day long, fairies and phantoms flying above your head? You must lose all touch with reality. How do you cope when you come back to the real world?
MIDNIGHT

Violet is fascinated with the magical worlds conjured up by the words and pictures of her favourite author, Casper Dream. If you could leave reality and visit a magical world all of your own, what would it look like? What kind of other-worldly creatures would you meet? On the facing page, can you give an artist's impression of this fantasy place?

JACQUELINE SAYS: I've always been very interested in fairies. I'm not talking about little-girly pink and pretty fairies prancing about on tiptoe – I mean strange, spooky weird creatures whirling though the air on gossamer wings. I love the Victorian fairy illustrations of Richard Dadd and John Anster Fitzgerald. I've got beautiful Edwardian picture books of Arthur Rackham's sepia fairies and W. Heath Robinson's goblins.

♥ 11 AUGUST ♥ ....

....

....

....

....

....

....

....

....

....

♥ 12 AUGUST ♥ ....

....

....

....

....

....

....

....

....

♥ 13 AUGUST ♥ ....

....

....

....

....

....

....

....

....

....

....

♥ 14 AUGUST ♥ ....

....

....

....

....

....

....

....

....

....

♥ 15 AUGUST ♥ ....

....

....

....

....

....

....

....

....

♥ 16 AUGUST ♥ ....

....

....

....

....

....

....

....

....

....

♥ 17 AUGUST ♥ ....

....

....

....

....

....

....

....

....

....

♥ 18 AUGUST ♥ ....

....

....

....

....

....

....

....

....

....

♥ 19 AUGUST ♥ ....
....
....
....
....
....
....
....
....
....

♥ 20 AUGUST ♥ ....
....
....
....
....
....
....
....
....
....

♥ 21 AUGUST ♥ ....

....

....

....

....

....

....

....

....

....

♥ 22 AUGUST ♥ ....

....

....

....

....

....

....

....

....

....

....

Let's GET CREATIVE . . .
With Furry Friends!

I put my hand out, trembling, and felt the softest fur,
like thistledown. I stroked tentatively, and the cat started
purring, rubbing her head under my hand, clearly telling
me to keep on stroking. I held her with one hand and
stroked with the other, from her head all the way
down her body to the tip of her long tail.

QUEENIE

During her stay at Miltree Hospital Elsie makes an extra
special friend – a beautiful big white cat called Queenie.
Do you have a favourite pet? If you don't, do you dream of
having an animal friend to call your own? On the facing
page, draw a picture of this special creature.

Hee hee
hee!

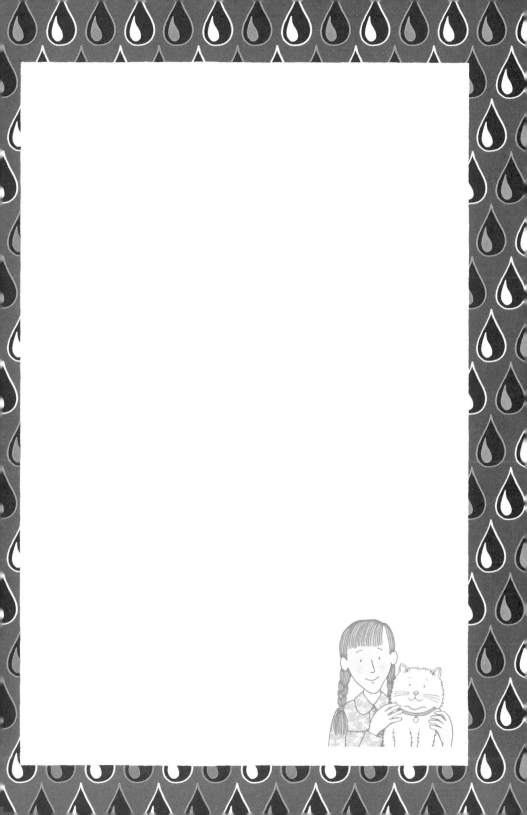

♥ 23 AUGUST ♥ ....
....
....
....
....
....
....
....
....
....

♥ 24 AUGUST ♥ ....
....
....
....
....
....
....
....
....
....
....

♥ 25 AUGUST ♥ ....

....

....

....

....

....

....

....

....

....

....

♥ 26 AUGUST ♥ ....

....

....

....

....

....

....

....

....

....

....

Let's GET CREATIVE . . . With Dolphin!

I wanted to do a pattern of marigolds as a border but Star had used up the orange already, so I turned the marigolds into roses and coloured them crimson. Red roses signify love. Marigold was very into symbols so I hoped she'd understand. Then on the back I did a great garland of red roses to signify a whole bunch of love and signed my name.

THE ILLUSTRATED MUM

Dolphin might not be so good at writing, but she's certainly a skilled artist – as her birthday card for her mother, Marigold, in *The Illustrated Mum* shows. Use this page to create a highly decorative design for a birthday card.

♥ 27 AUGUST ♥ ....

....

....

....

....

....

....

....

....

....

♥ 28 AUGUST ♥ ....

....

....

....

....

....

....

....

....

....

♥ 29 AUGUST ♥ ....

....

....

....

....

....

....

....

....

....

♥ 30 AUGUST ♥ ....

....

....

....

....

....

....

....

....

....

....

....

....

....

....

....

....

....

In *Candyfloss* Flora has a wonderful ride on a carousel horse
called Pearl. In the space below write ten words that sum up
the experience of going on your favourite fairground ride.

SEPTEMBER

Have you managed to keep up with your creative resolutions? Write about your progress below – you could even add some new ones to the list!

....
....
....
....
....
....
....
....
....
....
....
....
....
....

♥ 1 SEPTEMBER ♥ ....

....

....

....

....

....

....

....

....

....

♥ 2 SEPTEMBER ♥ ....

....

....

....

....

....

....

....

....

....

♥ 3 SEPTEMBER ♥ ....

....

....

....

....

....

....

....

....

♥ 4 SEPTEMBER ♥ ....

....

....

....

....

....

....

....

....

♥ 5 SEPTEMBER ♥ ....

....

....

....

....

....

....

....

....

♥ 6 SEPTEMBER ♥ ....

....

....

....

....

....

....

....

....

♥ 7 SEPTEMBER ♥ ....

....

....

....

....

....

....

....

....

....

....

♥ 8 SEPTEMBER ♥ ....

....

....

....

....

....

....

....

....

....

....

♥ 9 SEPTEMBER ♥ ....
....
....
....
....
....
....
....
....

♥ 10 SEPTEMBER ♥ ....
....
....
....
....
....
....
....
....
....

Let's GET CREATIVE . . .
With Clover and Hetty!

In *Clover Moon* Clover and her new friend Hetty Feather
enjoy the best ever tea party – they're treated to the tastiest
buns and cakes. Imagine the biggest, most delicious bun
you can think of. In the space below, list the ingredients
you would need to make this delectable dessert.

♥ 11 SEPTEMBER ♥ ....

....

....

....

....

....

....

....

....

....

♥ 12 SEPTEMBER ♥ ....

....

....

....

....

....

....

....

....

♥ 13 SEPTEMBER ♥ ....

....

....

....

....

....

....

....

....

....

♥ 14 SEPTEMBER ♥ ....

....

....

....

....

....

....

....

....

....

♥ 15 SEPTEMBER ♥ ....
....
....
....
....
....
....
....
....
....

♥ 16 SEPTEMBER ♥ ....
....
....
....
....
....
....
....
....
....
....

♥ 17 SEPTEMBER ♥ ....

....

....

....

....

....

....

....

....

....

♥ 18 SEPTEMBER ♥ ....

....

....

....

....

....

....

....

....

....

♥ 19 SEPTEMBER ♥ ....

....

....

....

....

....

....

....

....

....

♥ 20 SEPTEMBER ♥ ....

....

....

....

....

....

....

....

....

....

Let's GET CREATIVE . . .
With Places!

I reached the mulberry tree, I snatched a handful of berries and then rushed back. I scratched my hand on the tree and banged my shin badly climbing back over the gate but I had the mulberries safe in my hand. I crammed them into my mouth and the juice spurted over my tongue and I closed my eyes because it was just just just like being back at Mulberry Cottage.
THE SUITCASE KID

In *The Suitcase Kid*, following her parents' separation Andy feels caught between their two new homes. Always moving from one to the other, she wishes they could all be reunited in Mulberry Cottage where they used to live. Homes come in all different shapes and sizes – if you could live anywhere at all, what would your home look like? Would you live in a treehouse? Or in a warren like a rabbit, deep underground?

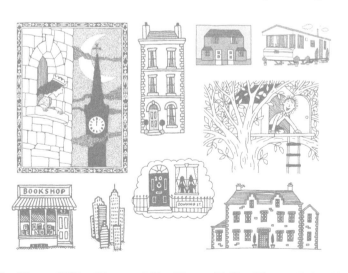

On this page draw the home of your dreams!

JACQUELINE SAYS: I know a lot of children think the true happy ending would be Andy's parents getting back together again but I didn't want to do that. I didn't want to give any child reader false hopes. I wanted to show Andy gradually learning to accept the situation, making new friends, growing a little, getting everything under control – until everything really is as easy as ABC.

♥ 21 SEPTEMBER ♥ ....

....

....

....

....

....

....

....

....

....

♥ 22 SEPTEMBER ♥ ....

....

....

....

....

....

....

....

....

....

♥ 23 SEPTEMBER ♥ ....

....

....

....

....

....

....

....

....

....

....

♥ 24 SEPTEMBER ♥ ....

....

....

....

....

....

....

....

....

....

....

♥ 25 SEPTEMBER ♥ ....

....

....

....

....

....

....

....

....

....

♥ 26 SEPTEMBER ♥ ....

....

....

....

....

....

....

....

....

....

♥ 27 SEPTEMBER ♥ ....

....

....

....

....

....

....

....

....

♥ 28 SEPTEMBER ♥ ....

....

....

....

....

....

....

....

....

♥ 29 SEPTEMBER ♥ ....

....

....

....

....

....

....

....

....

♥ 30 SEPTEMBER ♥ ....

....

....

....

....

....

....

....

....

Let's GET CREATIVE ...
With Opal!

I watched sugar syrup being mixed with gum and turned into a paste spread out on a marble table. It was punched out into little lozenges with a tin tube. I saw the syrup boiled extra vigorously until it turned brown, and was then sprinkled with slices of coconut to make dark coconut candy, cut into slabs when cold. I saw sugar mixed with great slabs of butter over the flames, the smell so sweet and rich my mouth watered.
OPAL PLUMSTEAD

Opal Plumstead's life changes for ever after her father is sent to debtor's prison. She has to earn money for her family by going to work in the Fairy Glen sweet factory. The factory makes all kinds of tooth-tingling sweets – can you invent one of your own? Describe what it would be like to eat your creation in the space below.

OCTOBER

Have you managed to keep up with your creative resolutions? Write about your progress below – you could even add some new ones to the list!

....
....
....
....
....
....
....
....
....
....
....
....
....
....
....
....

♥ 1 OCTOBER ♥ ....
....
....
....
....
....
....
....
....
....
....

♥ 2 OCTOBER ♥ ....
....
....
....
....
....
....
....
....
....
....

♥ 3 OCTOBER ♥ ....

....

....

....

....

....

....

....

....

....

♥ 4 OCTOBER ♥ ....

....

....

....

....

....

....

....

....

♥ 5 OCTOBER ♥

♥ 6 OCTOBER ♥

♥ 7 OCTOBER ♥ ....
....
....
....
....
....
....
....
....
....

♥ 8 OCTOBER ♥ ....
....
....
....
....
....
....
....
....
....

♥ 9 OCTOBER ♥ ....

....

....

....

....

....

....

....

....

....

♥ 10 OCTOBER ♥ ....

....

....

....

....

....

....

....

....

....

Let's GET CREATIVE . . .
On the Coast!

While we worked, I made up a story that we were three fairy princesses, each with her own castle. We took turns telling how our castles were decorated inside. Charlotte wanted marble throughout, with a four-poster bed with velvet curtains. Maisie wanted her walls studded with pearls, and she had a pearl dressing-table set to brush her long wavy princess hair. I chose coral for my palace, shiny and strange, in myriad patterns. I had a soft seaweed-green sofa stuffed with duck's down, where I reclined in a coral pink embroidered tea gown, writing my memoirs.

SAPPHIRE BATTERSEA

Hetty's imagination shows no sign of dulling in her second adventure, *Sapphire Battersea*, which takes her to the seaside. Like Hetty and her friends, have a go at imagining a seaside palace of your own. Which materials found on the beach would you use to build it? On the facing page, describe your coastal fortress.

♥ 11 OCTOBER ♥ ....

....

....

....

....

....

....

....

....

....

♥ 12 OCTOBER ♥ ....

....

....

....

....

....

....

....

....

....

♥ 13 OCTOBER ♥ ....

....

....

....

....

....

....

....

....

♥ 14 OCTOBER ♥ ....

....

....

....

....

....

....

....

....

....

....

♥ 15 OCTOBER ♥ ....

....

....

....

....

....

....

....

....

....

♥ 16 OCTOBER ♥ ....

....

....

....

....

....

....

....

....

....

♥ 17 OCTOBER ♥ ....

....

....

....

....

....

....

....

....

....

....

♥ 18 OCTOBER ♥ ....

....

....

....

....

....

....

....

....

....

....

♥ 19 OCTOBER ♥ ....

....

....

....

....

....

....

....

....

....

....

♥ 20 OCTOBER ♥ ....

....

....

....

....

....

....

....

....

....

....

....

♥ 21 OCTOBER ♥ ....
....
....
....
....
....
....
....
....
....

♥ 22 OCTOBER ♥ ....
....
....
....
....
....
....
....
....
....

Let's GET CREATIVE . . . With Beauty!

Mum and I were a real team when it came to cookie baking. Suddenly our bunny cookies were absolutely in demand.
COOKIE

In *Cookie* Beauty and her mum get really good at baking their bunny biscuits – Beauty's a dab hand at icing decorations too! In the space below, draw a tasty-looking cookie to rival Beauty's creations.

♥ 23 OCTOBER ♥ ....

....

....

....

....

....

....

....

....

....

♥ 24 OCTOBER ♥ ....

....

....

....

....

....

....

....

....

....

♥ 25 OCTOBER ♥ ....

....

....

....

....

....

....

....

....

....

♥ 26 OCTOBER ♥ ....

....

....

....

....

....

....

....

....

....

♥ 27 OCTOBER ♥ ....

....

....

....

....

....

....

....

....

....

♥ 28 OCTOBER ♥ ....

....

....

....

....

....

....

....

....

....

♥ 29 OCTOBER ♥ ....

....

....

....

....

....

....

....

....

♥ 30 OCTOBER ♥ ....

....

....

....

....

....

....

....

....

....
....
....
....
....
....
....
....
....

Hetty and Diamond take to the music-hall stage as the Little Stars. What would your Victorian music-hall stage name be? Draw it as it would appear on a poster in the space below.

NOVEMBER

Have you managed to keep up with your creative resolutions? Write about your progress below – you could even add some new ones to the list!

....

....

....

....

....

....

....

....

....

....

....

....

....

....

♥ 1 NOVEMBER ♥ ....
....
....
....
....
....
....
....
....
....
....
....

♥ 2 NOVEMBER ♥ ....
....
....
....
....
....
....
....
....
....
....

♥ 3 NOVEMBER ♥ ....
....
....
....
....
....
....
....
....

♥ 4 NOVEMBER ♥ ....
....
....
....
....
....
....
....

♥ 5 NOVEMBER ♥ ....

....

....

....

....

....

....

....

....

....

♥ 6 NOVEMBER ♥ ....

....

....

....

....

....

....

....

....

....

♥ 7 NOVEMBER ♥ ....

....

....

....

....

....

....

....

....

....

♥ 8 NOVEMBER ♥ ....

....

....

....

....

....

....

....

....

....

♥ 9 NOVEMBER ♥ ....

....

....

....

....

....

....

....

....

....

♥ 10 NOVEMBER ♥ ....

....

....

....

....

....

....

....

....

....

Let's GET SUPER CREATIVE . . .
With Marty!

I went back to my Marty Den, sat on my top bunk, and started
drawing an amazing new adventure of Mighty Mart. I didn't
mean to use a lot of the pencil. I was just going to do a quick
sketch. But then I had this great idea of giving Mighty Mart
giant springs in her feet, so she could jump — b-o-i-n-g ~
over rooftops and lampposts and trees. Drawing all these
astonishing feats took up three full pages in my sketchbook
— and most of Melissa's eye pencil.
THE WORST THING ABOUT MY SISTER

Cheeky Marty loves spending time creating all sorts of
thrilling adventures for her superhero alter ego Mighty Mart.
If you were a superhero, what would your name be? What
would your powers be? Which metropolis would you be
sworn to protect? Or would you hang out in the countryside?
And most importantly, what would your superhero
costume look like?

Use the facing page to create a page
from a comic about your superhero
avatar's adventures!

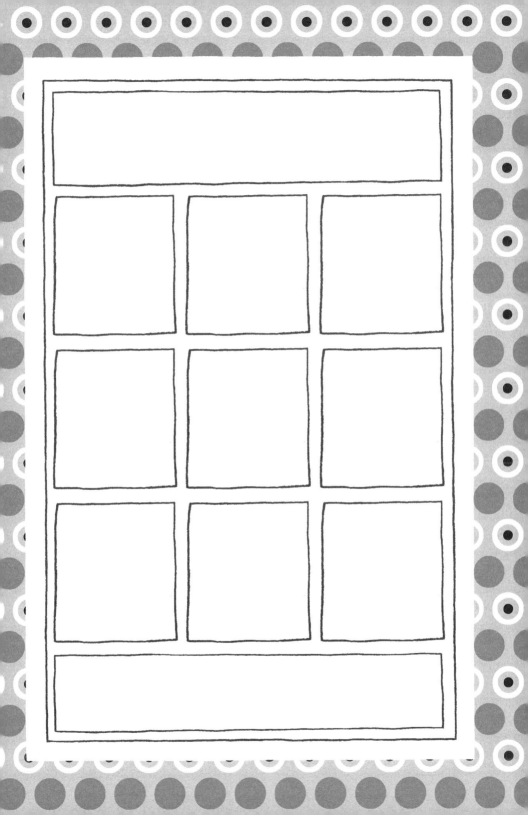

♥ 11 NOVEMBER ♥ ....
....
....
....
....
....
....
....
....

♥ 12 NOVEMBER ♥ ....
....
....
....
....
....
....
....
....

....

....

....

....

....

....

....

....

....

....

....

....

....

....

....

....

....

....

....

♥ 15 NOVEMBER ♥ ....
....
....
....
....
....
....
....
....
....

♥ 16 NOVEMBER ♥ ....
....
....
....
....
....
....
....
....
....
....

♥ 17 NOVEMBER ♥ ....
....
....
....
....
....
....
....
....

♥ 18 NOVEMBER ♥ ....
....
....
....
....
....
....
....
....

♥ 19 NOVEMBER ♥ ....

....

....

....

....

....

....

....

....

....

♥ 20 NOVEMBER ♥ ....

....

....

....

....

....

....

....

....

....

♥ 21 NOVEMBER ♥ ....

....

....

....

....

....

....

....

....

♥ 22 NOVEMBER ♥ ....

....

....

....

....

....

....

....

....

....

Let's GET CREATIVE . . . With Maps

Alice and I are best friends. I've known her all my life. That is absolutely true. Our mums were in hospital at the same time when they were having us. I got born first, at six o'clock in the morning on 3 July. Alice took ages and didn't arrive until four in the afternoon. We both had a long cuddle with our mums and at night time we were tucked up next to each other in little weeny cots.

BEST FRIENDS

Best friends Alice and Gemma are separated when Alice moves to Scotland with her family. Where does your best friend live? Use the facing page to create a map showing the route from your home to theirs. Your map can have as much detail in it as you like. Which landmarks are you going to include? What else do you need in your map to help you find the way?

JACQUELINE SAYS: One day at a big book signing, two little girls came up to me and announced together: 'We're best friends.' 'I'm just about to start writing a story about best friends,' I said. 'I haven't chosen their names yet. What are you two called?' 'Gemma and Alice,' they said. 'OK, that's what I'll call the girls in my new book,' I said, and I kept my promise. I do hope the real Gemma and Alice have read the book. I also hope they're still best friends!

♥ 23 NOVEMBER ♥ ....

....

....

....

....

....

....

....

....

....

....

♥ 24 NOVEMBER ♥ ....

....

....

....

....

....

....

....

....

....

....

♥ 25 NOVEMBER ♥ ....

....

....

....

....

....

....

....

....

♥ 26 NOVEMBER ♥ ....

....

....

....

....

....

....

....

....

♥ 27 NOVEMBER ♥ ....

....

....

....

....

....

....

....

....

♥ 28 NOVEMBER ♥ ....

....

....

....

....

....

....

....

....

♥ 29 NOVEMBER ♥ ....

....

....

....

....

....

....

....

....

....

♥ 30 NOVEMBER ♥ ....

....

....

....

....

....

....

....

....

....

....

DECEMBER

It's nearly the end of the year and almost time to make some new resolutions in January. Think about everything you've done this year – write down your proudest moments and achievements in the space below . . .

....

....

....

....

....

....

....

....

....

....

....

....

....

....

♥ 1 DECEMBER ♥ ....

....

....

....

....

....

....

....

....

....

♥ 2 DECEMBER ♥ ....

....

....

....

....

....

....

....

....

....

♥ 3 DECEMBER ♥ ....
....
....
....
....
....
....
....
....
....

♥ 4 DECEMBER ♥ ....
....
....
....
....
....
....
....
....

♥ 5 DECEMBER ♥ ....

....

....

....

....

....

....

....

....

....

♥ 6 DECEMBER ♥ ....

....

....

....

....

....

....

....

....

....

Let's GET CREATIVE . . .
At Christmas

I know it off by heart. I've made up a little tune and I sing it to myself every morning when I wake up and every night when I go to bed. I sing it softly in school. I sing it when I'm watching television. I sing it in the bath. I sing it on the toilet. I sing the punctuation and stuff too, like: 'Christ-mas, question mark. Lots of love, comma, Mum, kiss kiss kiss.' It's a very catchy tune. I might well be a song writer when I grow up as well as a famous novelist.
STARRING TRACY BEAKER

Use this spread to write the words to a brand-new Christmas song of your own. Will yours be a traditional-style carol, or will you write the lyrics to a pop*tastic* Christmas hit for your favourite band?

....

....

....

....

....

....

....

♥ 7 DECEMBER ♥ ....

....

....

....

....

....

....

....

....

....

♥ 8 DECEMBER ♥ ....

....

....

....

....

....

....

....

....

....

....

♥ 9 DECEMBER ♥ ....
....
....
....
....
....
....
....
....
....

♥ 10 DECEMBER ♥ ....
....
....
....
....
....
....
....
....
....

♥ 11 DECEMBER ♥ ....

....

....

....

....

....

....

....

....

....

♥ 12 DECEMBER ♥ ....

....

....

....

....

....

....

....

....

....

♥ 13 DECEMBER ♥ ....
....
....
....
....
....
....
....
....

♥ 14 DECEMBER ♥ ....
....
....
....
....
....
....
....
....
....

♥ 15 DECEMBER ♥ ....

....

....

....

....

....

....

....

....

....

♥ 16 DECEMBER ♥ ....

....

....

....

....

....

....

....

....

♥ 17 DECEMBER ♥ ....
....
....
....
....
....
....
....
....
....

♥ 18 DECEMBER ♥ ....
....
....
....
....
....
....
....
....
....

♥ 19 DECEMBER ♥ ....

....

....

....

....

....

....

....

....

....

♥ 20 DECEMBER ♥ ....

....

....

....

....

....

....

....

....

....

♥ 21 DECEMBER ♥ ....

....

....

....

....

....

....

....

....

....

....

♥ 22 DECEMBER ♥ ....

....

....

....

....

....

....

....

....

....

....

Make this spread into a time capsule and write a letter to yourself in a year's time. Which memories from this year would you want to remind yourself of? What are your hopes for yourself next year?

....
....
....
....
....
....
....
....
....
....
....
....
....
....
....
....
....
....
....
....

Keep this journal in a safe place and make
a reminder to open it in a year's time and
re-read this letter!

♥ 23 DECEMBER ♥ ....

....

....

....

....

....

....

....

....

....

♥ 24 DECEMBER ♥ ....

....

....

....

....

....

....

....

....

....

♥ 25 DECEMBER ♥ ....

....

....

....

....

....

....

....

....

....

♥ 26 DECEMBER ♥ ....

....

....

....

....

....

....

....

....

....

Have you enjoyed being creative this year? Use the space below to list your top ten most creative moments!

1. ....

2. ....

3. ....

4. ....

5. ....

6. ....

7. ....

8. ....

9. ....

10. ....

♥ 27 DECEMBER ♥ ....

....

....

....

....

....

....

....

....

♥ 28 DECEMBER ♥ ....

....

....

....

....

....

....

....

....

....

....

....

♥ 29 DECEMBER ♥ ....

....

....

....

....

....

....

....

....

....

♥ 30 DECEMBER ♥ ....

....

....

....

....

....

....

....

....

....

....

....

....

....

....

....

....

....

....

....

In *Starring Tracy Beaker* Tracy has lots of ideas about what she should get for Christmas. What would you get for Tracy this year? Draw a picture of your gift all wrapped up with a lovely ribbon!

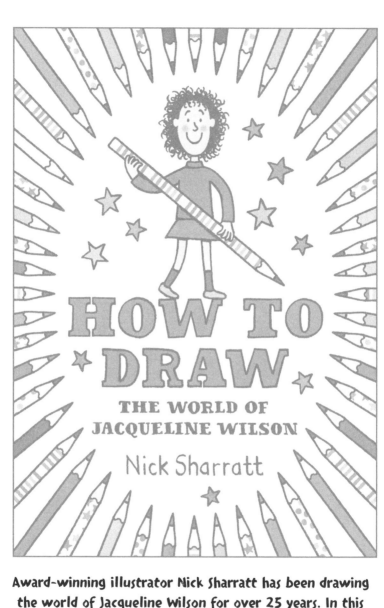

HOW TO DRAW

THE WORLD OF JACQUELINE WILSON

Nick Sharratt

Award-winning illustrator Nick Sharratt has been drawing
the world of Jacqueline Wilson for over 25 years. In this
handy guide, get his tips and tricks on how to recreate
your favourite characters, including Tracy Beaker
and Hetty Feather, and much more!

Jacqueline Wilson

Colouring Book

Illustrated by
Nick Sharratt

Lose yourself in this beautiful colouring book,
bursting with Nick Sharratt's inspirational illustrations
of Jacqueline Wilson's larger-than-life characters!

Visit Jacqueline Wilson's Storyland for more creative ideas . . .

If you've enjoyed being creative with the activities in this book, why not visit the Storyland on Jacqueline Wilson's website?

You can write your own stories, choose your own book covers, enter writing competitions, share your books with friends, check out books in the public library, review each other's books and much more!

Choose from one of five story themes: Adventure, Friendship, Holiday, Victorian or Romance!

For more information, visit Jacqueline's brilliant website

www.jacquelinewilson.co.uk